Malaga

The Alcazaba from the Paseo del Parque

Málaga, Spain – 2-Day Tour from the Moors to Picasso

By Deborah Cater

Copyright © 2018 by Unanchor LLC

All rights reserved. No part of this publication may be reproduced, distributed, or transmitted in any form or by any means, including photocopying, recording, or other electronic or mechanical methods, without the prior written permission of the publisher, except in the case of brief quotations embodied in critical reviews and certain other noncommercial uses permitted by copyright law. For permission requests, write to the publisher, addressed "Attention: Permissions Coordinator," at the address below.

All maps are copyright OpenStreetMap contributors. Please visit www.openstreetmap.org/copyright for more information.

Address:

Unanchor Press
P.O. Box 184
Durham, NC 27701
www.unanchor.com

Ordering Information:

Quantity sales. Special discounts are available on quantity purchases by corporations, associations, and others. For details, contact the publisher at the address above.

Orders by U.S. trade bookstores and wholesalers. Please contact Unanchor at hello@unanchor.com, or visit http://www.unanchor.com.

Printed in the United States of America

Unanchor is a global family for travellers to experience the world with the heart of a local.

Table of Contents

INTRODUCTION..9
DAY 1...13
  9:30 am -- Roman Theatre and Alcazaba................13
  11:30 am -- Castillo Gibralfaro................................16
  12:30 pm -- English Cemetery................................18
  1:00 pm -- La Malagueta Bullring to the Beach...........20
  2:00 pm -- Siesta/Lunch..22
  4:00 pm -- Málaga Cathedral..................................24
  4:35 pm -- Picasso Museum...................................26
  8:00 pm -- Night-time in Málaga..............................27
DAY 2...30
  9:30 am -- Málaga Market.....................................30
  10:10 am -- Museum of Popular Arts and Customs
  (Museo de Artes y Costumbres Populares)...................34
  11:05 am -- Temple of the Sacred Heart......................37
  11:35 am -- Carmen Thyssen Museum........................39
  1:00 pm -- Lunch at El Pimpi via the Plaza de la
  Constitución..41
  3:00 pm -- Siesta/Free Time....................................45
  5:20 pm -- Contemporary Art Museum.......................49
  8:00 pm -- Dinner in Málaga...................................50
ABOUT THE AUTHOR..52
  Deborah Cater..53
UNANCHOR WANTS YOUR OPINION...55
OTHER UNANCHOR ITINERARIES...56

Introduction

=============

Details include the brand new galleries - The Pompidou and The Russian Museum - which are helping to really put Málaga on the map.

Málaga is one of the oldest cities in the world with its history dating back to the Phoenicians in the eighth century BCE. It is an elegant, vibrant and interesting city and has been the home and birthplace of many famous people including Pablo Picasso and Antonio Banderas.

Are you a lover of art and history?

Then this is the itinerary for you! The itinerary focuses on the area around the port and the old town of Málaga. Day One takes in the east side and Day Two the west side. Both days have a mixture of art, museums and sights. Included in the itinerary are:

Museum of Popular Arts and Customs

This quaint museum is often missed, which is the loss of others but not you! With open displays shown in a Moorish-influenced old tavern, you get to see the Málaga of yesteryear for only 4 Euros.

Málaga Market

Although I have recommended restaurants and tapas bars in the itinerary sometimes a picnic is just as good. This market with its fresh produce is where the locals do their shopping. Grab fresh bread, some olives, cheese and oil, and create your own feast - or simply enjoy the sights and smells of the real Málaga.

The English Cemetery

A little known fact: Málaga was the first place in Spain to have a cemetery for non-Catholic Christians. The first day's itinerary takes you to these beautiful restful gardens.

These are just tasters of a delicious 2 days. Also included are:

- The Pablo Picasso Museum
- The Carmen thyssen museum
- Málaga Cathedral
- Alcazaba and Roman Theatre
- Castel Gibralfaro
- The Bullring
- Contemporary Art Gallery
- Restaurant Recommendations

The itinerary has been split into two days allowing ample time for the sights to be taken in without rushing. Each sight is accompanied with pictures and a walking map to ensure a stress-free experience.

Time has also been given for siestas and long lunches – the Spanish way! In the height of the summer, the temperatures can reach 40˚C and walking during that heat is not advised and can be very tiring. In addition, a number of shops and sights close between the hours of 2pm and 4pm. The hottest part of the day therefore has been given over to food and relaxation.

To help make your stay as enjoyable as possible I have included a number of useful Spanish words and phrases in the Appendix.

Still unsure?

My e-mail is in the itinerary and I am always happy to help.

I can guarantee that if art and history interest you, you will have a wonderful vacation in this fascinating city!

Day 1

=============

9:30 am -- Roman Theatre and Alcazaba

- **Price:** EUR €2.20 (for a single adult)
- **Duration:** 1 hour and 30 minutes
- **Address:** Calle Alcazabilla

The day starts outside the Teatro Romano or Roman Theatre. The entrance to the theatre is on the left as you look at it, whilst the entrance to the Alcazaba is to the right of the theatre, about 100 metres away.

The remains of the Roman Theatre sit below the entrance to the Alcazaba and can be viewed from the pavement but it is much better to get into the seats to get a real sense of atmosphere. There is an interesting display in the entrance area which gives information on the Roman occupation and the excavation of the theatre. The theatre is free.

To the right of the theatre is the Alcazaba, a Moorish fortified palace which dates from the ninth century AD. It is located in the foothills of Mount Gibralfaro and links to the Gibralfaro Castle on top of the hill by a rocky corridor called The Corach, which sadly you can no longer walk up. Muslim art and gardens create a wonderful place to absorb Málaga's history.

Local's tip: The palace ruins are on a slope but do make every effort to explore the site, especially the Moorish garden with fountain.

11:00 am -- Walk to Castillo Gibralfaro

- **Price:** FREE
- **Duration:** 30 minutes

From the Alcazaba it is possible to walk up the steep hill to the castle. From the entrance/exit to the Alcazaba follow the wall round to the right and follow the small road upwards. On the left you will see steps to a footpath that winds up the hill – take this path and climb to the top.

If you feel unable to make the walk to the Castle, and in the summer heat it might be difficult, then catch the number 35 bus from the 3rd bus stop on the Paseo del Parque (see map below). The black line is the route from the theatre/Alcazaba to the bus stop; the blue line is the route the bus takes. The bus takes around 25 minutes to get the castle. The bus costs €1 and runs every 50 minutes which may put your itinerary out slightly but not so that you will miss any opening times.

11:30 am -- Castillo Gibralfaro

- **Price:** EUR €2.20 (for a single adult)
- **Duration:** 30 minutes
- **Address:** Castillo de Gibralfaro, s/n 29016 Málaga, Spain

The Arab word Yabal means hill and the Spanish work for lighthouse is far; Gibralfaro derives from these two words. As part of the Moorish rule of Málaga the castle was built during the reign of Yusuf I (1333-1354). The castle was used as a military base until 1925 but it has deteriorated over the years and mainly walls remain. There is a museum on-site which is included in the entrance fee.

If you are fit enough the walk is worth it. The views from here are just fantastic of the city and out across the port and Mediterranean Sea.

Local's tip: There is a kiosk at the castle bus-stop, which is not over-priced, where you can buy water and snacks.

12:00 pm -- Walk to the English Cemetery

- **Price:** FREE
- **Duration:** 30 minutes

From the castle you can either walk down the hill, or take the number 35 as you choose. The bus passes outside the English Cemetery; ask the driver for the Cementerio Inglés and he will let you know when to get off.

Walking route from the castle to the cemetery.

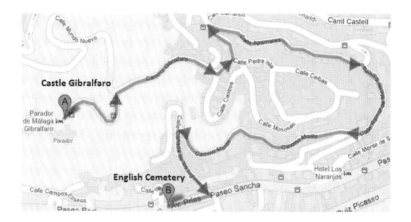

12:30 pm -- English Cemetery

- **Price:** EUR €3.00 (for a single adult)
- **Duration:** 30 minutes
- **Address:** Avenida Pries

The English Cemetery is so named as it was created by an Englishman and for some time the land was owned by the British Government. It is in fact a cemetery for non-Catholic Christians and was the first one to be opened on the Spanish mainland. Before the foundation of the cemetery, the disposal of non-Catholics was a rather macabre and gruesome 'ceremony'. Internment had to happen outside of daylight hours and the body had to be taken to the shore and buried in an upright position. The bodies were at the mercy of the sea and scavenging animals – not nice to put it mildly.

The cemetery has some lovely headstones and they are attractive gardens in their own right. Buried within the cemetery are the remains of the Captain, Chief Engineer and 60 seamen of the Imperial German Navy Sail Training Ship "Gneisenau" wrecked outside Malaga harbour on 16 December 1900. The Hispanist Gerald Brenan, his wife Gamel Woolsey, the Spanish poet Jorge Guillen, and the Finnish author Aarne Haapakoski are also interred here.

1:00 pm -- La Malagueta Bullring to the Beach

- **Price:** FREE
- **Duration:** 1 hour
- **Address:** Plaza del Toros

It is a short walk (5 minutes) along the Paseo Reding from the English Cemetery to Málaga's bullring, La Malagueta in the Plaza del Toros. From the bullring it is only another 5 to 10 minutes to Muelle Uno.

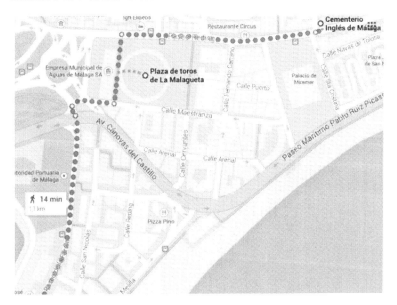

La Malagueta was built in 1874, by the architect Joaquín Rucoba and the first fight took place on 11 June 1876. In 1976, the site was declared an Historic Artistic Monument, and declared an Official Site of Cultural Interest in 1981.

The bullfighting season runs from April to September, a little earlier if Easter falls in March. The highlights for fights are during Holy Week (Semana Santa) and the Feria in August. The bullring is open to the public during the fighting season and is free to walk in and look around.

Málaga has a number of beaches which run along the length of the Paseo Maritimo. During the main holiday season (April to October), the chiringuitos on the beaches are very popular; however, on this side of the city they have been updated from beach huts to restaurants and have lost their atmosphere and do not provide such good value for money.

2:00 pm -- Siesta/Lunch

- **Price:** FREE
- **Duration:** 1 hour and 45 minutes
- **Address:** Restaurant of your choice Muelle Uno

Restaurants and bars offer traditional Spanish food to quick snacks and Asian cuisine. This is also an option for the evening meal.

The lighthouse and Muelle Uno (harbor) where there are many bars and restaurants.

Local's tip: *The beach bars are either closed or offer a limited menu and service during the off-season. The restaurants in the port and town generally provide the same service all year round.*

3:45 pm -- Walk to Málaga Cathedral

- **Price:** FREE
- **Duration:** 15 minutes

The walking directions below are from the port/Muelle Uno restaurants to the Cathedral along the Paseo Espana.

Cross over into the central area and walk through the gardens for respite from the sun and a pretty stroll.

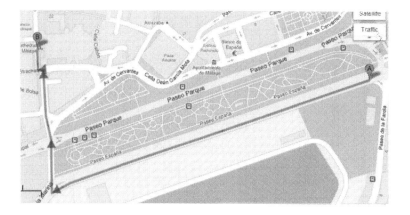

4:00 pm -- Málaga Cathedral

- **Price:** EUR €5.00 (for a single adult)
- **Duration:** 30 minutes
- **Address:** Calle Molina Lario

The afternoon gets under way with a trip to the cathedral. Known as the Cathedral of the Incarnation, the cathedral is located where the Mosque-Aljama stood during the eight centuries of Muslim rule.

Construction on the church started in 1528 and continued until the 18th century. It remained unfinished with only one tower completed which gives the cathedral its popular name, "The Manquita" - one-armed.

The cathedral is quite dark inside, which I find atmospheric. Some of the statues are eerily lifelike.

4:30 pm -- Walk to the Picasso Museum

- **Price:** FREE
- **Duration:** 5 minutes

From the cathedral it is a short 3 minute walk through some of Málaga's twisting streets to the Museo Picasso. Remember to look up as sometimes the best architecture is above your head with ornate iron balconies and interesting windows.

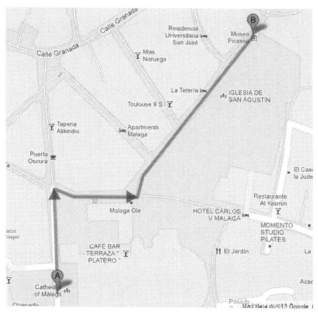

4:35 pm -- Picasso Museum

- **Price:** EUR €8.00 (for a single adult)
- **Duration:** 1 hour and 25 minutes
- **Address:** Palacio de Buenavista, Calle San Agustín

The price above is for the permanent and temporary collections.

Museo Picasso Málaga was created in response to Pablo Picasso's own desire for his work to be present in the city where he was born on 25 October 1881. The museum covers eight decades of Picasso's works, including sculpture and video.

You have to appreciate Picasso's work to appreciate this art gallery. I have visited it several times and I am finally starting to understand where he is coming from! Read the information that is painted onto the walls in the rooms, it helps with the understanding.

Local's tip: Avoid queuing by purchasing your tickets in advance. You can then walk to the front of the queue. Tickets have an entrance time. Advance ticket sales at www.unientradas.es

8:00 pm -- Night-time in Málaga

- **Price:** EUR €20.00 (for a single adult)
- **Duration:** 3 hours

The evening is free for you to explore the streets of the Old Town or stroll along the promenades that run all along the coast. The Spanish are known for talking their promenade of an evening and the older generation will often be seen making their way along the front at a leisurely pace.

Restaurants are open from around 1pm through to midnight, sometimes later. Málaga has a mix of restaurants from small tapas bars in side streets to larger restaurants but very few chains or franchises – a good thing in my book.

If you want atmosphere there is not much point in going out earlier then 8pm. In the summer the Spanish wait for the heat of the day to dissipate slightly before venturing out. At weekends they will be out, old and young, until the early hours of the morning.

As well as the new restaurants and bars that line the harbor, Muelle Uno, there are the more traditional restaurants in the Old Town. I have eaten in all of the restaurants below and recommend each of them for different reasons. They offer something a little bit different in each case but with a flavor of Spain, particularly in the case of El Tapeo de Cervantes.

El Tapeo de Cervantes combines traditional tapas with new creative offerings and is the most popular restaurant in the city. It has a warm and welcoming atmosphere, excellent service and a superb range of wines and beers.

Calle Cárcer, 8 Tel: 952 609458
www.eltapeodecervantes.com

Vino Mio is a modern restaurant, run by a Dutch restaurateur, in the square outside of the Cervantes Theatre. Here you get a more continental menu with dishes such as kangaroo, Spanish pork and French duck confit. It is reasonably priced, and at lunchtime you can get a 3 course Menu del Dia for €12,50. In the evenings there is a Flamenco show from 8pm to 9.30pm. After midnight the restaurant becomes a lounge bar.

Plaza Jerónimo Cuervo, 2 Tel: 952 60 90 93
http://www.restaurantevinomio.com

Pepa y Pepe is a bar offering tapas at a reasonable price. The young crowd can be found here grabbing a bite to eat before heading off to the nightclubs. It gets busy so don't expect overly attentive waiting staff. Tapas range between €2 and €5.

Calle Calderia, 9

Day 2

=============

9:30 am -- Málaga Market

- **Price:** FREE
- **Duration:** 30 minutes
- **Address:** Calle Anatazaras

Day 2 starts with a taste of Málaga life followed by how life was lived in the province in years gone by. The art experiences also range from the old way of life to the very modern. The walk takes you through some of Málaga's old streets with a mix of architecture and through the modern Plaza de la Constitución.

After the long walks of Day 1, this is easier on the legs with plenty of time for contemplating the art and enjoying the flavour, quite literally, of Málaga at the renowned El Pimpi bar and restaurant.

On the corner of Calle Anatazaras, in a beautiful iron building with large stained glass window is Málaga's food market. Apart from Mondays when the fish counters are closed, each of the colourful modern stalls is full of fresh, local produce.

The vegetables and fish are displayed like pieces of art. If you want to buy some snacks to see you through the day, this is the place to do so. The locals buy their produce here so it is not overly priced.

Local's Tip: You can taste the olives and nuts before you buy, so don't be afraid to ask. (¿Puedo probar esto?) There are also local olive oils – a healthy way to add flavour to your salad and other dishes.

10:00 am -- Walk to the Museum of Popular Arts and Customs

- **Price:** FREE
- **Duration:** 10 minutes

It is roughly a 6 minute walk from the Market to the Museum. Head west along Calle Atarazanas before turning left along Plaza Arriola. This brings you out by the river. Follow the road, keeping the river on your left, until you come to the museum on your right. The entrance is at the rear of the building.

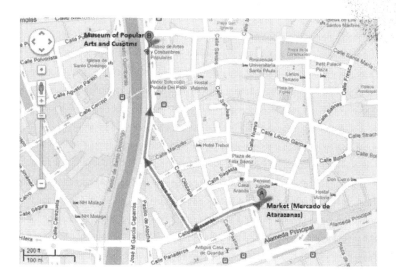

10:10 am -- Museum of Popular Arts and Customs (Museo de Artes y Costumbres Populares)

- **Price:** EUR €4.00 (for a single adult)
- **Duration:** 50 minutes
- **Address:** Pllo Santa Isabel, 10

This is a quaint little museum that is housed in a 17th century building that used to be the Victoria Tavern. The museum recovers and conserves the ethnographic heritage of the region. The displays show the day-to-day life of Málaga and its province through local customs and activities.

I love this museum for its displays that are not behind glass, allowing you to feel involved with the experience.

The building wraps around an Andalucían courtyard, filled with flowers and sunlight. This is typical Málaga architecture of the time, with the house spread over two floors and all the rooms leading off of the galleries that surround the internal courtyard.

11:00 am -- Walk to the Temple of the Sacred Heart

- **Price:** FREE
- **Duration:** 5 minutes

From the museum it is a three minute walk to the Temple of the Sacred Heart. Head east on Calle García Briz toward Calle Muro de Puerta Nueva. Turn left onto Calle Muro de Puerta Nueva. Turn right onto Calle Compañía. About 100 metres along is the small square of Plaza de San Ignacio on your left. The church is tucked into this tiny square.

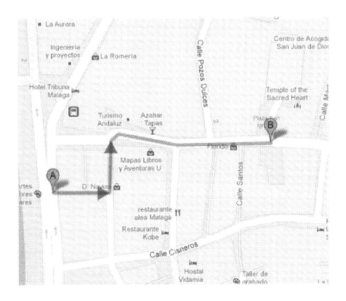

11:05 am -- Temple of the Sacred Heart

- **Price:** FREE
- **Duration:** 25 minutes
- **Address:** Plaza de San Ignacio off of Calle Compañía

This is an architecturally stunning church that sits back from the street and can easily be overlooked. That would be sacrilege!

Built in 1920, in the Neo-Gothic style, the two towers of the church flank a wonderful rose window. The interior of the church is also neo-Gothic in style with large paintings of the saints Francis and Ignacius.

Local's Tip: *If the priest is in, he is a very friendly man to chat to; he knows a little English and will tell you about the church.*

The neo-Gothic facade of the church squeezed into a tiny square.

11:30 am -- Walk to the Carmen Thyssen Museum

- **Price:** FREE
- **Duration:** 5 minutes

Turn left out of the Church's square and in less than a minute from the church you arrive at the doors to the Carmen Thyssen Museum.

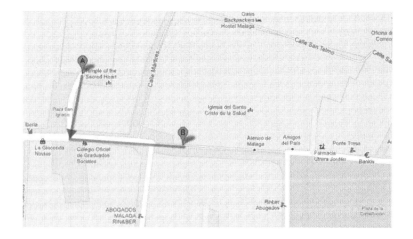

11:35 am -- Carmen Thyssen Museum

- **Price:** EUR €6.00 (for a single adult)
- **Duration:** 1 hour and 25 minutes
- **Address:** Calle Compañía

As with the Picasso Museum there are from time to time temporary exhibitions in the Carmen Thyssen Museum. The price above is for the permanent collection only. A combined ticket to the Permanent Collection and a temporary exhibition is €9. Entry is free on Sundays after 5pm.

It's not just the art collection that traces Spain's heritage, the building itself is a mix of architectural styles and times. The main building that constitutes the museum was the Palacio de Villalón which has undergone a number of alterations over the centuries. When the museum took over they uncovered and restored some of the buildings gems. Look at the carved wooden ceilings in the entrance foyer.

The art collection covers the Old Masters and nineteenth century Spanish painting with the emphasis on the art of Andalucía. From depictions of traditional Spanish customs and life the collection progresses to Romanticism and Realism schools of art – always remaining firmly within Spain.

Take a close look at the pictures on the ground floor that show Málaga centuries ago to get an idea of just how much the city has changed. The scary looking figures in dark robes with pointed hats are part of the religious bodies that process through the towns and cities of Spain at high religious festivals such as Easter. There are also light-hearted pictures of flamenco dancing and inebriated hombres in bars!

Local's Tip: *The museum can get busy during the high-season so beat the queues by buying your tickets online. http://entradas.carmenthyssenmalaga.org/museos.aspx*

1:00 pm -- Lunch at El Pimpi via the Plaza de la Constitución

- **Price:** EUR €10.00 (for a single adult)
- **Duration:** 2 hours
- **Address:** Calle Granada

With your appetite for local customs and art hopefully sated for the time being, it's now time to curb the physical hunger! A leisurely stroll from the Carmen Thyssen Museum to El Pimpi takes you through the Plaza de la Constitución and along the Calle Granada.

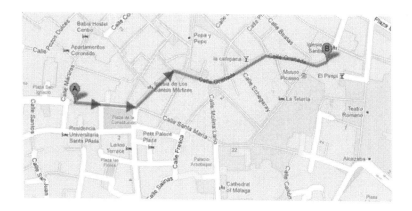

The Plaza de la Constitución, as many plazas in Spain were, was named as such after the Constitution of Spain was signed in 1978, following the end of Franco's dictatorial rule. In front of the bakery and coffee shop, which can be seen to the right of the rather funky Christmas tree, are bronze plaques set into the ground. These are images of the front pages of Spanish newspapers celebrating the constitución.

Plaza de la Constitución on a sunny December day with the Cathedral's tower in the background.

Local's tip: *In your free time, if you would like a traditional thick hot chocolate or a cup of coffee and pastry the bakery cum coffee house is a brilliant place to take a break (NOT Café Central but the small yellow building that is behind the bronze plaques). The pastries are fresh and can be selected from the counter downstairs. The coffee shop is upstairs. It is small but if you can, squeeze onto one of the three tables on the balcony and watch the people in the Plaza below.*

Local's Tip: Don't rush and miss some of the lovely side streets that ooze character.

El Pimpi is near the Roman Theatre, bringing you back to where you started the itinerary on day 1. With typical malagueñan decor and a variety of rooms and terraces in which to eat and drink, El Pimpi offers the opportunity to enjoy local wines and fine food. Some of the barrels in the main restaurant are signed by famous people such as Picasso, Antonio Banderas and the Duchess of Alba.

Local's tip: Try the fino sherry for a refreshing lunchtime tipple. The Salmorejo soup is a cold tomato soup, thicker than a Gazpacho that is both filling and refreshing on a summer's day.

Local's tip: The terrace offers good views of the Alcazaba but there is a 15% supplemental charge for service there.

Calle Granada, 62 Tel: 952 22 89 90 http://www.elpimpi.com

3:00 pm -- Siesta/Free Time

- **Price:** FREE
- **Duration:** 2 hours

A long leisurely lunch and the heat of a summer's day means that a siesta may be required. If you don't fancy a snooze, then a dip in the sea could be just the ticket. Of course you could just lengthen the lunch experience.

Apart from the major stores, the smaller shops will close for siesta so shopping at this time would be only a semi-experience.

5:00 pm -- Walk to Contemporary Art Museum

- **Price:** FREE
- **Duration:** 20 minutes

If you stayed at El Pimpi for a well-earned break then the route map will take you from there to the Contemporary Art Museum. It is about a 15-20 minute walk.

Head out of El Pimpi through the entrance that overlooks the Roman Theatre; turn right and walk past the theatre and the Alcazaba along the edge of Plaza Aduana. Crossing over the road towards the Paseo España, keep right and cross over again on to Plaza de la Marina then a slight kink left and right onto Calle Vendeja which then becomes Calle Linaje. At the end of Calle Linaje, turn left onto Avenida Comandante Benítez and the museum will be in front of you.

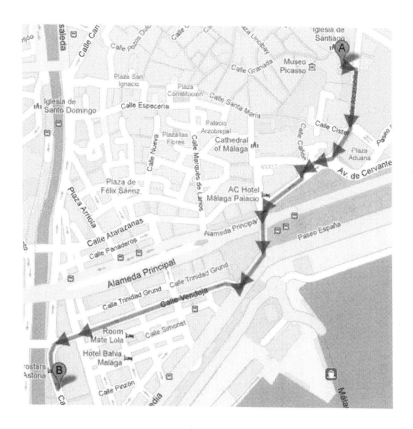

5:20 pm -- Contemporary Art Museum

- **Price:** FREE
- **Duration:** 40 minutes
- **Address:** Avenida Comandante Benítez

Picasso may be Málaga's most famous artist but the city has not rested on its laurels and the Centro de Arte Contemporáneo opened its doors in 2003. This is a truly modern art experience and attracts some of the world's best-known contemporary artists.

I think Picasso would have approved of the city of his birth carrying on his tradition of ground-breaking art.

8:00 pm -- Dinner in Málaga

- **Price:** EUR €30.00 (for a single adult)
- **Duration:** 3 hours

As with Day One there is no better way to finish a day than a stroll and good food.

El Trillo is just off of the main shopping street, Larios, and offers typical Spanish fayre. Attentive staff are happy to help with menu translations. Inside the restaurant looks like a typical meson decorated with bottles and pictures. Main courses are priced between €8 and €25 depending on your choice of dish. Calle de Don Juan Diaz, 4; Tel: 952 603 920 grupotrillo.es

If you had indulged in a large lunch at El Pimpi, you may wish to enjoy a lighter evening meal or tapas for which I can recommend those from Day One - **El Tapeo Cervantes** which combines traditional tapas with new creative offerings and is the most popular restaurant in the city. It has a warm and welcoming atmosphere, excellent service and a superb range of wines and beers. Calle Cárcer, 8 Tel: 952 609458 www.eltapeodecervantes.com

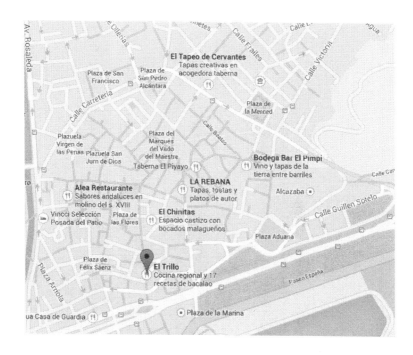

About the Author

Deborah Cater

Thank you for purchasing the itinerary. Please send any feedback, suggestions, problems or questions to deborah@dccopywriting.com Also, I would be grateful if you could rate this itinerary on www.Unanchor.com

I am originally from England but I have been living in the Málaga province since 2010. I have fallen in love with the city of Málaga and spend as much time there as possible. It has developed from a rundown airport city to the wonderful place it is today, and it continues to improve. I hope that you find it as interesting and enchanting as I do.

Feel free to drop me a line if you have any questions about the city or province of Málaga, deborah.uk@libero.it

Twitter: @DeborahCater

Blog: http://citychronicles-deborahcater.blogspot.com.es/

Unanchor
Chief Itinerary Coordinator

Unanchor wants your opinion

Your next travel adventure starts now. A simple review on Amazon will grant you and a travel buddy, friend, or human of your choosing any of the wonderful Unanchor digital itineraries for free.

What a deal!

Leave a review:

- http://www.amazon.com/unanchor

Collect your guides

- Send an email to reviews@unanchor.com with a link to your review.
- Wait with bated breath.
- Receive your new travel adventure in your inbox!

Other Unanchor Itineraries

Africa

- One Day in Africa - A Guide to Tangier
- Johannesburg/Pretoria: A 4-Day South Africa Tour Itinerary
- Cape Town - What not to miss on a 4-day first-timers' itinerary

Asia

China

- Beijing Must Sees, Must Dos, Must Eats - 3-Day Tour Itinerary
- 2 Days in Shanghai: A Budget-Conscious Peek at Modern China
- Shanghai 3-Day Tour Itinerary

India

- 3-Day Budget Delhi Itinerary
- Delhi in 3 Days - A Journey Through Time
- 3 Days Highlights of Mumbai
- A 3-Day Tryst with 300-Year-Old Kolkata
- Kolkata (Calcutta): 2 Days of Highlights

Japan

- Nozawa Onsen's Winter Secrets - A 3-Day Tour
- Tour Narita During an Airport Layover
- 3-Day Highlights of Tokyo

Singapore

- Family Friendly Singapore - 3 Days in the Lion City
- The Affordable Side of Singapore: A 4-Day Itinerary
- A First Timer's Guide to 3 Days in the City that Barely Sleeps - Singapore
- Singapore: 3 Fun-Filled Days on this Tiny Island

Rest of Asia

- Between the Skyscrapers - Hong Kong 3-Day Discovery Tour
- Art and Culture in Ubud, Bali – 1-Day Highlights
- Go with the Sun to Borobudur & Prambanan in 1 Day
- 3 Days in the Vibrant City of Seoul and the Serene Countryside of Gapyeong
- Manila on a Budget: 2-Day Itinerary
- A 3-Day Thrilla in Manila then Flee to the Sea
- The Very Best of Moscow in 3 Days
- Saint Petersburg in Three Days
- The Two Worlds of Kaohsiung in 5 Days
- 72 Hours in Taipei: The All-rounder
- The Ins and Outs of Bangkok: A 3-Day Guide
- Girls' Weekend in Bangkok: Shop, Spa, Savour, Swoon
- Saigon 3-Day Beyond the Guidebook Itinerary

Central America

Mexico

- Your Chiapas Adventure: San Cristobal de las Casas and Palenque, Mexico 5-Day Itinerary
- Mexico City 3-Day Highlights Itinerary
- Everything to see or do in Mexico City - 7-Day Itinerary
- Todo lo que hay que ver o hacer en la Ciudad de México - Itinerario de 7 Días
- Cancun and Mayan Riviera 5-Day Itinerary (3rd Edition)

Europe

France

Paris

- Paris to Chartres Cathedral: 1-Day Tour Itinerary
- A 3-Day Tour of Mont St Michel, Normandy and Brittany
- Paris 4-Day Winter Wonderland
- The Best of Paris in One Day
- Paris Foodie Classics: 1 Day of French Food
- Paris 1-Day Itinerary - Streets of Montmartre
- Paris 3-Day Walking Tour: See Paris Like a Local
- Paris for Free: 3 Days
- Art Lovers' Paris: A 2-Day Artistic Tour of the City of Lights

Greece

- Athens 3-Day Highlights Tour Itinerary

- Chania & Sfakia, Greece & Great Day Trips Nearby (5-Day Itinerary)
- Day Trip From Thessaloniki to Kassandra Peninsula, Halkidiki, Greece
- 2-Day Beach Tour: Travel like a Local in Sithonia Peninsula, Halkidiki, Greece
- Thessaloniki, Greece - 3-Day Highlights Itinerary

Italy

- Discover Rome's Layers: A 3-Day Walking Tour
- A 3-Day Tour Around Ancient Rome
- 3 Days of Roman Adventure: spending time and money efficiently in Rome
- A Day on Lake Como, Italy
- Milan Unknown - A 3-day tour itinerary
- Landscape, Food, & Trulli: 1 Week in Puglia, the Valle d'Itria, and Matera
- 3-Day Florence Walking Tours
- Florence, Italy 3-Day Art & Culture Itinerary
- See Siena in a Day
- Three Romantic Walks in Venice

Netherlands

- Amsterdam 3-Day Alternative Tour: Not just the Red Light District
- Amsterdam Made Easy: A 3-Day Guide
- Two-day tour of Utrecht: the smaller, less touristy Amsterdam!

Spain

- Málaga, Spain – 2-Day Tour from the Moors to Picasso
- Mijas - One Day Tour of an Andalucían White Village
- Two-Day Tour in Sunny Seville, Spain
- FC Barcelona: More than a Club (A 1-Day Experience)
- 3-Day Highlights of Barcelona Itinerary
- Ibiza on a Budget - Three-Day Itinerary
- Three days exploring Logroño and La Rioja by public transport
- Best of Valencia 2-Day Guide

United Kingdom
England
London

- 3-Day London Tour for Olympic Visitors
- London's Historic City Wall Walk (1-2 days)
- London 1-Day Literary Highlights
- The 007 James Bond Day Tour of London
- An Insider's Guide to the Best of London in 3 Days
- Done London? A 3-day itinerary for off the beaten track North Norfolk
- London's South Bank - Off the Beaten Track 1-Day Tour
- Low-Cost, Luxury London - 3-Day Itinerary
- London for Free :: Three-Day Tour
- London's Villages - A 3-day itinerary exploring Hampstead, Marylebone and Notting Hill

Rest of England

- Bath: An Exploring Guide - 2-Day Itinerary
- 2-Day Brighton Best-of Walks & Activities

- Bristol in 2 Days: A Local's Guide
- MADchester - A Local's 3-Day Guide To Manchester
- One Day in Margate, UK on a Budget

Rest of United Kingdom

- History, Culture, and Craic: 3 Days in Belfast, Ireland
- The Best of Edinburgh: A 3-Day Journey from Tourist to Local
- Two-Day Self-Guided Walks - Cardiff

Rest of Europe

- 3 Days in Brussels - The grand sites via the path less trodden
- Zagreb For Art Lovers: A Three-Day Itinerary
- 3-Day Prague Beer Pilgrimage
- Best of Prague - 3-Day Itinerary
- 3 Days in Helsinki
- Weekend Break: Tbilisi - Crown Jewel of the Caucasus
- 2 Days In Berlin On A Budget
- A 3-Day Guide to Berlin, Germany
- 3 Days in Dublin City - City Highlights, While Eating & Drinking Like a Local
- Krakow: Three-Day Tour of Poland's Cultural Capital
- Best of Warsaw 2-Day Itinerary
- Lisbon in 3 Days: Budget Itinerary
- Braşov - Feel the Pulse of Transylvania in 3 Days
- Lausanne 1-Day Tour Itinerary

Middle East

- Adventure Around Amman: A 2-Day Itinerary
- Amman 2-Day Cultural Tour
- 3 Days as an Istanbulite: An Istanbul Itinerary
- Between the East and the West, a 3-Day Istanbul Itinerary

North America

Canada

- Relax in Halifax for Two Days Like a Local
- The Best of Toronto - 2-Day Itinerary
- An Insider's Guide to Toronto: Explore the City Less Traveled in Three Days
- Toronto: A Multicultural Retreat (3-day itinerary)

United States

California
Los Angeles

- Los Angeles On A Budget - 4-Day Tour Itinerary
- Los Angeles 4-Day Itinerary (partly using Red Tour Bus)
- Downtown Los Angeles 1-Day Walking Tour
- Sunset Strip, Los Angeles - 1-Day Walking Tour
- 2-Day Los Angeles Vegan and Vegetarian Foodie Itinerary
- Los Angeles Highlights 3-Day Itinerary
- Hollywood, Los Angeles - 1-Day Walking Tour

San Francisco

- San Francisco Foodie Weekend Itinerary
- San Francisco 2-Day Highlights Itinerary
- The Tech Lover's 48-Hour Travel Guide to Silicon Valley & San Francisco

Rest of California

- Orange County 3-Day Budget Itinerary
- Beverly Hills, Los Angeles - 1-Day Tour
- Wine, Food, and Fun: 3 Days in Napa Valley
- Beyond the Vine: 2-Day Napa Tour
- Palm Springs, Joshua Tree & Salton Sea: A 3-Day Itinerary
- Beer Lovers 3-Day Guide To Northern California
- RVA Haunts, History, and Hospitality: Three Days in Richmond, Virginia
- Best of the Best: Three-Day San Diego Itinerary
- Three Days in Central California's Wine Country

Florida

- 2 Days Exploring Haunted Key West
- 3-Day Discover Orlando Itinerary
- Three Days in the Sunshine City of St. Petersburg, Florida

Hawaii

- Lesser-known Oahu in 4 Days on a Budget
- Local's Guide to Oahu - 3-Day Tour Itinerary
- Tackling 10 Must-Dos on the Big Island in 3 Days

Illinois

- Chicago Food, Art and Funky Neighborhoods in 3 Days
- 3-Day Chicago Highlights Itinerary
- Famous Art & Outstanding Restaurants in Chicago 1-Day Itinerary
- 6-Hour "Layover" Chicago

Kansas

- The Best of Kansas City: 3-Day Itinerary
- Day Trek Along the Hudson River
- Wichita From Cowtown to Air Capital in 2 Days

Massachusetts

- Navigating Centuries of Boston's Nautical History in One Day
- Rainy Day Boston One-Day Itinerary
- Boston 2-Day Historic Highlights Itinerary

New York

- Brooklyn, NY 2-Day Foodie Tour
- A Local's Guide to Montauk, New York in 2 Days - From the Ocean to the Hills
- Weekend Day Trip from New York City: The Wine & Whiskey Trail
- Day Trip from New York City: Mountains, Falls, & a Funky Town
- Lower Key, Lower Cost: Lower Manhattan - 1-Day Itinerary
- Jewish New York in Two Days

- Hidden Bars of New York City's East Village & Lower East Side: A 2-Evening Itinerary
- New York City - First Timer's 2-Day Walking Tour
- New York Like A Native: Five Boroughs in Six Days
- 3-Day Amazing Asian Food Tour of New York City!
- New York City's Lower East Side, 1-Day Tour Itinerary
- Weekend Tour of Portland's Craft Breweries, Wineries, & Distilleries
- Day Trip from New York City: Heights of the Hudson Valley (Bridges and Ridges)

Pennsylvania

- A Laid-Back Long Weekend in Austin, TX
- 3 Day PA Dutch Country Highlights (Lancaster County, PA)
- Two Days in Philadelphia
- Pittsburgh: Three Days Off the Beaten Path

Rest of United States

- Alaska Starts Here - 3 Days in Seward
- The Best of Phoenix & Scottsdale: 3-Day Itinerary
- Tucson: 3 Days at the Intersection of Mexico, Native America & the Old West
- The Best of Boulder, CO: A Three-Day Guide
- Louisville: Three Days in Derby City
- A Local's Guide to the Hamptons 3 Day Itinerary
- New Haven Highlights: Art, Culture & History 3-Day Itinerary
- Atlanta 3-Day Highlights
- Savannah 3-Day Highlights Itinerary

- La Grange, Kentucky: A 3-Day Tour Itinerary
- New Orleans 3-Day Itinerary
- Baltimore: A Harbor, Parks, History, Seafood & Art - 3-Day Itinerary
- Summer in Jackson Hole: Local Tips for the Perfect Three to Five Day Adventure
- Las Vegas - Gaming Destination Diversions - Ultimate 3-Day Itinerary
- Las Vegas on a Budget - 3-Day Itinerary
- Cruisin' Asbury like a Local in 1 Day
- Girls' 3-Day Weekend Summer Getaway in Asheville, NC
- Five Days in the Wild Outer Banks of North Carolina
- Family Weekend in Columbus, OH
- Ohio State Game Day Weekend
- Portland Bike and Bite: A 2-Day Itinerary
- Three Days Livin' as a True and Local Portlander
- Corpus Christi: The Insider Guide for a 4-Day Tour
- An Active 2-3 Days In Moab, Utah
- The Weekenders Guide To Burlington, Vermont
- Washington, DC in 4 Days
- Washington, DC: 3 Days Like a Local
- A Day on Bainbridge Island

Oceania
Australia

- Two Wheels and Pair of Cozzies: the Best of Newcastle in 3 Days
- A Weekend Snapshot of Sydney

- Sydney, Australia - 3-Day **Best Of** Itinerary
- The Blue Mountains: A weekend of nature, culture and history.
- Laneway Melbourne: A One-Day Walking Tour
- Magic of Melbourne 3-Day Tour
- A Weekend Snapshot of Melbourne
- An Afternoon & Evening in Melbourne's Best Hidden Bars
- Best of Perth's Most Beautiful Sights in 3 Days

New Zealand

- Enjoy the Rebuild - Christchurch 2-Day Tour
- The Best of Wellington: 3-Day Itinerary

South America
Peru

- A 1-Day Foodie's Dream Tour of Arequipa
- Arequipa - A 2-Day Itinerary for First-Time Visitors
- Cusco and the Sacred Valley - a five-day itinerary for a first-time visitor
- Little Known Lima 3-Day Tour

Rest of South America

- An Insider's Guide to the Best of Buenos Aires in 3 Days
- Buenos Aires Best Kept Secrets: 2-Day Itinerary
- Sights & Sounds of São Paulo - 3-Day Itinerary

Unanchor is a global family for travellers to experience the world with the heart of a local.

Made in the USA
San Bernardino, CA
11 July 2018